Peace In The Storms of Life

30 Day Devotional

Sherry Tarlton

Haley Tarlton

W. R. PARKS
Hershey, PA

Paperback ISBN: 978-0-88493-069-3

The Kings James Version of the bible is quoted in this book.

Cover artwork: Jesus Sermon on the Mount by Carl Bloch

Publisher: William R. Parks

Hershey, Pennsylvania

wparkspublishing@aol.com

www.WRParks.com

Twitter: www.twitter.com/WParksPublisher

Facebook: www.facebook.com/wparkspublishing

Acknowledgements

I want to thank my wonderful husband, Terry Tarlton, for all his hard work, patience.and encouragement.

I want to thank a special friend, Ray Sierra. For all his prayers and encouragement.

I want want to thank my family and friends for all their prayers and support.

And a big thank you for all those who shared their testimony.

My Story

I helped my three year old son out of his highchair closed the Bible that I was reading and placed it on the table. I walked over to the patio door to watch my husband till up our garden, admiring his strong body and determination to complete the job.

I prayed and asked God to give me the courage to ask him to go to church. I took a deep breath and approached Terry.

"We are going to church, would you like to come?"

He threw his work gloves on the ground and stomped across the grass to where I was standing. I could see the anger in his eyes that my new found faith provoked. His face turned red and his body shook with anger.

He began shouting "How many times do I have to tell you, Sherry? I don't need your God! It is only a religious crutch!" His face now in mine, he yelled and pointed to the house. "Who do you think bought you that house?"

My voice quivered and I whispered "You did."

"Who bought you that car?"

"You did."

"That's right" he said. "I did, not your God." He raised his arms up in the air and proclaimed, "As long as I have this strong body I will never need your God." He smacked his hands on his legs, "And these two strong legs are all I need. I don't need your God. If you are so weak and need that crutch, that's fine, but don't bring that religious garbage home to me."

He gave me one last glance as he turned and walked away. I went to comfort my son who was scared because of his daddy's rage. I picked Shawn up and held him close. I told him that everything would be okay. I whispered a prayer, grabbed my Bible off the table and headed for the car. After I had put Shawn in his car seat, I hesitated before shifting into gear leaning my head against the steering wheel. I wanted to calm myself down so I could drive to church.

The next day, I went to the doctor and discovered I was two months pregnant. I was so excited and could not wait to tell Terry that he was going to be a daddy again.

I prepared a special candle light dinner and waited for Terry to come home. I watched the candle grow dim and the food started getting cold. I began wondering where Terry could be. He was always on time. My silent thought was shattered by the ringing of the phone. It was the hospital informing me that Terry had been involved in an car accident. Thankful Shawn was at a neighbor's house, I grabbed my keys and purse and rushed to the hospital. When I got there a nurse took me to see Terry. He was awake and asked me about Shawn. I did not have time to answer as they rushed him away to surgery.

While I was waiting for Terry to get out of

surgery, I went to check on the other man involved in the accident. When I asked to see him or his family the nurse told me that he had already been released. I blinked. "Already?"

I said. "Wasn't he hurt?" Her eyes met mine and I could see the pity in them. "I am grateful for that," I said.

The nurse took my hand,"Don't feel sorry for him" she said. "He was drunk and driving without a license. He was driving on the wrong side of the road and hit your husband's car head on. The man walked away without a scratch while your husband is in surgery."

I did not know what to say. All I could do was walk away. I felt numb as I walked back to the waiting room anxious to hear word about Terry.

When I got there, a highway patrolman was waiting for me. He explained the accident happened just like the nurse had said.

Our conversation was interrupted by the doctor entering the room. He sat me down before speaking. Terry was bleeding and they could not find where the blood was coming from.

"Ma'am, I'm sorry" he said "But I don't think your husband will live through the night. Do you have family that you could call to stay with you?"

I burst into tears. The highway patrolman put his arm around my shoulder. "I will stay with you until your family comes," he said. I thought of our two children and begged God not to take their daddy.

The next morning the doctor came to talk with me.

"Your husband survived the night and he has a good chance of making it. However if he does live he will never walk again." He proceeded to tell me that Terry's right leg was broken in seven places and the other leg was mangled. Both of his feet had been crushed.

Terry remained in intensive care for three weeks fighting for his life. He was not receiving any treatments as they were waiting for the outcome. After he was stabilized and able to be moved to a private room, the doctor finally assured me Terry would live. I was so thankful for those words. They put him in a body cast and said he would be in the cast for three months. I knew it would be a long long road to recovery.

It gave me comfort to know Shawn was being taken care of. Each night I would call him and he would cry, wanting to know if he could come home and see his daddy. I would tell him we would all be together soon. I would hang up the phone with my son's cries echoing in my ears. I would spend a lot of time in the garden, as it was the one place I could find comfort. As I pulled weeds, I would cry and pray.

Months later an ambulance brought Terry home in a body cast from his armpits to his toes. My family brought Shawn home and we were all together at last. My family was great about coming to check on us. We could not have made it without their never-ending love and financial support. I gave birth to our second son, Barry and our family was totally complete now.

My faith was tested beyond all that I could imagine.

I had a newborn, a three year old and an atheist in a body cast. It was my responsibility to pay bills and provide food. We could not get help from the government since we owned our home.

One day I received a shut-off notice from the electric company. I had heard that the government would pay your bill if you needed help. You just had to bring in your shut-off notice and come to their office. So I bundled up the boys and stood in the long line.

The elderly lady behind me kept coughing and swaying from one foot to the other. She said she was very sick and felt like she was going to faint. Finally when it was my turn to go in, I felt sorry for the lady. "Why don't you go ahead of us " I suggested. She thanked me and went inside.

When she came out, the government worker was with her. "I'm sorry folks, but we are out of funds" he announced and I felt like I had been slapped in the face.

I held Shawn's small hand, cradled Barry close and headed home. I thought "That's what I get for trying to be kind."

Later that week, after I had spent our last penny

on bills, I stared at the empty cabinets. I knew my children needed food and I didn't have any to give them. God's Word had taught me that He was in charge of all things, so I cried out for help. I reminded Him of what His Word said and how He promised to meet our needs. I prayed for a long time until I felt compelled to check my coat pocket. I found twenty dollars in my pocket. Overjoyed, I hurried off to the store to buy food for my family.

I picked up a pound of hamburger, thinking of the chili I was going to make when the grocer took the meat from my hands. He wrote a much lower price on the package and handed it back to me. I thanked him and put it in my cart. The man smiled and picked up another package, marked it down and gave it to me. Them he did the same with another. He said, "I don't know why I'm doing this." I smiled and said"I do." I had all I need to make the chili, and I had enough to buy bread and peanut butter. I also had enough to buy my baby some formula. We had enough food to last for two weeks.

The following week was Easter. I wanted to go to church on Easter Sunday as a family. Terry had graduated from a body cast to leg casts. The doctors said that he would never walk and would have to continue in a wheelchair.

On Easter Sunday I was getting the boys ready for church and praying for the courage to ask Terry to join us. I found the courage to ask him and he shocked me by saying yes.

We sat in the back of the crowded church. Terry's wheelchair was parked in the aisle by my seat. Shawn sat on his lap and I held Barry. The choir sang and it was beautiful. Then a group called The Messengers sang a special. It was called One Day Too Late. It was about a wife and her children going to Heaven and leaving her husband behind. I looked at Terry and saw the tears flowing down his face.

After church, he took my hand and said "Sherry, that's me. I'm not going to Heaven with you." He patted his legs that has been casts for two years. "How could God forgive me?" he asked.

I looked at him and said "Maybe God spared your life so that you could learn that He is God. He is in control of the universe instead of you.

My husband was saved that Easter Sunday when he gave his life to Jesus. Now thirty five years later, I climb in the passenger side of the car and smile as Terry closes the door for me. He hobbles around to the driver's side clutching a cane in one hand and a Bible in the other. He will never have those two strong legs again but he has so much more. He will never walk without pain, but against the doctor's predictions he is walking. His face shines with a peace and joy that he never had before the accident.

What about me? Well I praise God every day for Terry and for being his two strong legs

Day One

2 Thessalonians 3:18

The Lord Himself gives you peace.

We will always have challenges as long as we live here on earth.

A friend of mine once told me. "It's not what you go through in life but how we handle ourselves while going through the situation."

When the troubles of this world come crashing down around you remember that God is in the midst of the storm.

God promised to never leave or forsake us. He is the Lord of Peace and is able to give us peace in every situation.

God's Peace allows us to rest in the middle of every storm.

God's Peace cannot be found in the world. It can only be found in God.

If you are in a storm today call upon God and He will hear you. Ask Him for His Peace.

I pray that you will experience God's Blessing through His amazing Peace.

Sherry

Day One

Humor For The Day.

I once had a pet duck. It became ill and I took it to the doctor. When I entered the doctor's office my duck was very still. The doctor put my duck on the examining table and listened to it's heart. The doctor informed me that my duck was dead.

I told the doctor that I wanted some test's ran on my duck. Maybe he had just fainted.

The doctor left the room and came back with a labrador retriever. The dog jumped up on the table and sniffed the duck. He looked at the doctor and shook his head.

The doctor took the dog out and came back with a cat.

The cat jumped up on the exam table and sniffed the duck. The cat looked at the doctor and shook his head.

The doctor left the room with the cat.

The doctor came back in the room and said "all the tests confirmed your duck is dead," and then handed me a bill for $ 120.

I was shocked and yelled, "$120 to tell me my duck is
    dead."

The doctor replied. "Well it would have only been $ 20, but you asked for a lab test and a cat scan."

Day One

Health Tips For The Day

Health benefits of drinking water helps maximize physical performance, affects energy levels and brain function.

Just losing 2% of your body's water content can impair your physical performance.

Water is critical for digestion. Staying hydrated also helps to eliminate toxins from the body, which can damage the gut by causing irritation and inflammation.

You should drink lot's of water every day.

The rule of thumb for how much water you should drink is to take half your body weight and drink that amount in ounces.

Tea, coffee or sodas do not count, only water. When you drink anything with caffeine you should drink a glass of water for every caffeine drink you consume.

Today drink plenty of water. It is good for your health.

Day Two

Proverbs 16:24

Pleasant words are like a honeycomb, sweetness to the soul, and health to the bones.

The words that we say are very important. We can use our words for any reason. We can use words to build
self-esteem and encourage others. Words can also be used to tear down or discourage them. I sometimes have a hard time thinking before I speak.

We often hear people say, " if you don't have anything nice to say, then don't say anything." I disagree with that statement. I love and agree with Kid President saying
" if you can't think of anything nice to say, then your not thinking hard enough." That is so true.

If we think hard enough we can find something good to say. We should always try to see the good in every person. I know that some people get on our nerves, but we should still try to see the good in them.

When someone messes up and makes a mistake we shouldn't make fun of them. We should encourage them and let them know that we all make mistakes. Let them know that no one is perfect and you love them anyway. We all make mistakes from time to time but what matters is what we do after the mistake.

James tells us to bridle our tongues, but we never fully bridle our tongues. We can ask God to empower us to hold our tongues. We can ask for His help to let us think before we speak. He can give us the strength to work harder to use our words to build up others.

Every day we should be looking for the good in others and say kind words to encourage them. You never know, it just might make someone's day.

Haley

Day Two

Humor For The Day

Why do we tell actors to " break a leg" ?

Because every play has a cast.

Yesterday I saw a man spill all his scrabble pieces on the road.

I asked him " What's the word on the street" ?

Once my dog, Lily, ate all the scrabble tiles.

For days she kept leaving messages all over the house.

Day Two

Health Tip For The Day

Shallow breathing may be harmful to your health. If you are unsure whether you are a shallow breather do this.

Place your hands against your abdomen beneath your rib cage and exhale.

Take a deep breath and follow the movements of your hand. Your hands should move up and down.

Shallow breathing affects your whole body. It may cause stress, headache and back and neck pain.

According to The Mayo Clinic, shallow breathing may play a role in lung and heart functions.

Deep breathing is very beneficial to your body. Deep breathing is a great exercise to practice.

Get comfortable and inhale deeply through your nose,
allowing your abdomen to fill with air, gently expanding out. Exhale by relaxing and releasing all the air through your nose.

Day Three

Ephesians 6:10

Finally my brethren, be strong in the Lord, and in the power of His might.

One beautiful summer day my husband took me to his favorite fishing spot. We threw our lines in the water and waited for the fish to bite. It was a slow day for fishing and we were not getting any bites.

My husband, Terry, kept switching from one bait to another but the fish would not take the bait.

I could not help thinking that that is what the devil does to Christians.

He tries different baits or techniques to pull us away from God. He tries to keep us focused on ourselves and our problems.

Sometimes he tries to overwhelm us with a busy schedule. The devil will use any bait possible to keep our minds and hearts on ourselves.

We can not focus on God while we are all wrapped up in ourselves.

The devil will try to trap us in living and thinking like the world. As Christians, we need to be aware of the temptations of the devil.

We need to overcome his snares by standing on God's Word. We cannot fight the devil in our strength. He is only defeated by the power of God's Word.

Sherry

Day Three

Humor For The Day

I spent the first twelve years of my teaching career,
teaching hearing impaired children.

One fall I was teaching on a thanksgiving unit, about the Pilgrims and the Mayflower Ship arriving at Plymouth Harbor in 1620. After explaining why the Pilgrims wanted to come to America, I asked the question
"does any one know the name of the ship the Pilgrims
came in?"

Jimmy one of my very shy students, excitedly raised his hand indicating he knew the answer. I was so thrilled that he wanted to share in the discussion. I called on him and said " Jimmy tell the class the name of the ship the Pilgrims arrived in at Plymouth Rock."

Jimmy replied with confidence "The Love Boat". The Love Boat was an American comedy television series,
set on a luxury passenger cruise ship.

Day Three

Health Tips For The Day

Oats are among one of the healthiest grains on earth. They are a great source of important vitamins, minerals, fiber and antioxidants. Studies show that oats and oatmeal have many health benefits . These include weight loss, lower blood sugar levels and a reduced risk of heart disease.

Steel cut oats may be a better choice for those looking for better control of their blood sugar. Steel cut oats are slightly higher in fiber. They also have a lower glycemic index making them the best choice for blood sugar control.

The next time you are trying to decide between the two oats, it might be your best bet to consider what you want to use them for.

Trying out a cookie recipe, go for the rolled oats. Craving a hearty breakfast, then steel cut oats might be the better option.

Day Four

Philippians 4:4
Rejoice in the Lord, and again I say rejoice.

This summer my family and I have been working on a project. We were building a house for some goats that I was getting. While working with some carpentry equipment my Papaw cut off part of his finger.

We were all worried about him. We were concerned about what painful surgeries he might have to go through. Papaw was not worried. He never complained or said one negative word. He set a wonderful example for me and all his grandkids.

A friend of the family said "happiness is based on happenings, but true joy is always there no matter what."
That is what I saw in my Papaw, true joy.

I want to have that kind of joy, not the kind that fades with my circumstances. I want the true joy that only God can give.

Paul and Silas are another great example of joy. The Bible tells us that they were thrown into prison and shackled for telling others about God.

They still prayed and sang unto the Lord, even while they were shackled in prison.

I want to be like that, sold out for Jesus. I want to be joyful in every situation, not happy but joyful.

Haley

Day Four

Humor For The Day.

What do computers eat for lunch ?

    Micro chips

What happens to a toad's car when it breaks down?

    It gets toad

If you have 13 apples in one hand and 12 oranges
in the other hand , what do you have ?

    Big hands

Why couldn't Cinderella play soccer ?

    She kept running away with the ball.

Day Four

Health Tips For The Day

According to Healthy Living, berries are among some of the world's most powerful superfoods. They are very nutritional , delivering many health benefits.

Berries are considered one of the best superfoods because they are low in calories and they contain a high level of antioxidants.

Antioxidants are compounds that help fight off free radicals and strengthen your immune system.

In addition to protecting your cells, they may help reduce the risk of disease.

Berries are easy to find. They are found in almost every grocery store.

Day Five

2 Timothy 1: 7

For God hath not given us the spirit of fear, but of power, and love and of a sound mind.

I can remember a time in my life when I was controlled by fear.

I often found myself being a people pleaser or being fearful of what tomorrow would bring. I was so fearful that I developed panic attacks.

I was so thankful to discover that I could be free from fear.

I learned to trust God's unconditional love.

1 John 4:18 Tells us that perfect love casteth out fear and God's love is perfect.

I know that we are living in a time of unrest. The world seems to be full of violence and every state is plagued with the virus.

I am not suggesting that we don't need to be concerned, but we don't have to let fear dominate our lives.

I just want to encourage you if you are overwhelmed by a situation and it is stealing your joy and peace and making you worry.

I just want you to know that there is an antidote for you.

It is simply trusting in God's word and believing His promises. He promised that He would never leave or forsake us.

Sherry

Day Five

Humor For The Day

My two nieces , Jan and Brenda went to the store with their mom. She bought them a Clark candy bar to share.
Jan broke the candy bar in two but one side was bigger than the other.
So Jan took a bite of the bigger piece and said "there Brenda, now it's even."
Brenda exclaimed "that's not fair."

On my granddaughter, Haley's, third birthday she came to my house for a tea party.
When Haley came into the house I said "Haley your birthday is finally here."
Haley looked all around, shrugged her shoulders and said "but I don't see it."

Day Five

Health Tips For The Day

All greens are not created equal. Some greens are more nutritious than others.

Celery has the least nutritional value.

Green and red leaf lettuce is more nutritious. They are very low in calories. They are also very high in potassium and vitamin A and K.

My favorite lettuce is the butter lettuce, also called Boston or Bib lettuce.

The leaves are higher in potassium and iron than the green leaf lettuce.

Romaine lettuce is another healthy choice for a salad.
It is packed full of vitamins.

The Swiss chard, kale and spinach are also good healthy choices for salad.

They all pair well with beets, berries and apples for a very delicious and healthy salad.

Day Six

Psalms 17:6
I call on You God, for You will answer me.

Just recently, I had been contemplating whether
or not to play softball. I prayed and asked God if
He wanted me to play softball or did He have other
plans for me.

I love playing ball. It gives me a chance to share
Jesus with the other girls. I also like playing ball
because it is a great way to meet new friends. I
really love the game but it is so expensive.

I prayed and asked God " If You want me to play
this year then You need to provide the money."

After praying like this about a week my uncle
came to visit. We were talking about me playing
softball and I explained the money situation. He
not only offered to pay for my softball but
volunteered to coach.

His offer did come with an understanding that I
would make him cookies until the season was over.
I thought that was a good trade off because I love
to bake.

This may seem small to you but it was a big deal
to me.

I know that there are a lot of people in the world
worrying about a lot bigger things than softball but
I find great comfort knowing that God cares about
the small things also.

He cares about everything in our lives, big or

small. Prayer will change things.

The next time you need something, remember God is only a prayer away.

Haley

Day Six

Humor For The Day

Silas, my little brother, overheard my mom and dad talking about the news on TV. They talked about the news and other events that were happening that day.

As Silas was listening he heard them talking about the earthquakes and the tsunami that hit Japan.

My little brother's ears perked up and he asked "How can a stick of salami kill people." "Did they hit people over the head with it until they died."

He thought they said salami not tsunami.

Day Six

Health Tips For The Day

When my granddaughter,Haley, was younger she
wanted to raise chickens for the eggs. She also
wanted a goat for the milk. She never got the goat
but She did raise chickens for a few years.

I'm glad she did because she learned a lot about
chickens and eggs.

The eggs from the chickens are considered to be
one of the most complete protein sources found in a
food.

Due to the amino acid in eggs they are used as a
checking point on how much proteins other foods
have.

Eggs are also a good source of vitamin A, vitamin
B1, Vitamin D, and Niacin.

Eggs have been a good source of our nutrition for
a long time.

So, eat your eggs.

Day Seven

Ephesians 1:3
  Blessed be the God and Father of
our Lord Jesus Christ

  We are to bless The Lord. You might ask "How do
we bless The Lord?"
  We bless The Lord when we share Him with
others. We bless Him when we talk to others about
how good He is and what wonderful things He has
done in our lives. We need to tell others how God
loves them and forgives them of all their sins.
  Share how that when God forgives them He
removes their sin forever. We are here on Earth for
a few short years but eternity is forever.
  God has blessed us. Why don't we try to bless God
and share our faith with someone today.

Sherry

Day Seven

Humor For The Day

When I was about 10, my brother, Bill, and I were playing in the rain.

My boots got stuck in mud and I could not move. Bill tried and tried to pull me out but couldn't. Bill said " I'll walk home and get some help."

I waited for a very long time for help to arrive, but help did not come.

So I pulled my feet out of the boots and walked home barefoot.

When I got home my brother was watching TV. He had forgotten to get me help.

We are both grown now but he is still forgetful. Just the other day he took a shower and forgot to take his socks off.

Day Seven

Health Tips For The Day

My friend, Ray, introduced me to the best tasting and healthiest hot chocolate.

It has three times more Vitamin E than spinach. It has seven times more Vitamin C than oranges.

It is heart healthy and good for indigestion. It is packed full of antioxidants and many other nutrients. It is all natural and has only 1.8g of sugar. It can be purchased in almost any health food store or purchased online.

It is Moringa Hot Chocolate!

Thank you Ray for introducing me to this wonderful hot chocolate.

Day Eight

1 Corinthians 10:13
No temptation has overtaken you that except what is common to man, and God is faithful, He will not let you be tempted beyond what you can bear.

Temptation is a trap of the world and satan. Temptation is what satan uses to pull us away from God. If we endure temptation without falling into the trap then God will bless us.

When temptation knocks at the door then just don't open the door.

The Bible tell us that blessed is the man who endures temptation, he will receive a crown of life. Temptation is a testing of one's faith. It is not a sin to be tempted. Jesus himself was tempted. When we give in to the temptation is when it becomes a sin.

We have a choice with temptation, we can chose to say no or to give in to it. It is not easy to resist temptation.

James tells us that we must endure hardships like a good soldier. I love the thought of being a soldier for God.

We could learn some lessons from the soldiers in the military. They learn how to prepare for the battle. They are taught to stay focused on the mission.

As Christians we are in God's Army and always

at war with temptation. If we want to win the battle we must be prepared. God's word will prepare us to fight against temptation.

Jesus used scriptures to help Him overcome temptation. We can win the battle against temptation if we use scriptures and stay focused on Jesus.

Haley

Day Eight

Humor For The Day

When I was about four I went on a fishing trip with Mimi and Grandpa.

We were all having a wonderful time catching fish. Grandpa was catching big fish but I was only catching little fish that we had to throw back into the lake. I tried very hard to catch a big fish.

Once I thought I had a big fish but it was only My Mimi.

I could not cast very good at four. I had thrown my line out and thought it had gone into the lake but instead it caught on Mimi's lips.

She kept saying "Haley stop, don't move, stand still."

Grandpa had to remove the hook from her lips.

It was still a fun day even though I did not catch a big fish.

Day Eight

Health Tip For The Day

My family loves to exercise. We go on long hikes in the woods. We love riding our bikes. Sometimes we will lift weights. I am so glad that we exercise as a family.

Exercise has many health benefits. It is not only good for you physically but mentally as well. It may even help you live longer. It is good for your muscles and bones.

Exercise may improve your mood and make you feel happier. It can also increase your energy level. I know after exercise I feel better.

Exercise is very good for your body. So be good to your body and exercise.

Day Nine

John 15:5

I am the vine, ye are the branches: he that abideth in Me, and I in him, the same bringeth forth much fruit: for without Me you can do nothing.

Sometimes when we face trials in our lives we often focus more on the problem instead of on God. Sometimes we even try to solve our problems by ourselves. Then when we realize we can't solve them on our own we become discouraged and depressed.

The longer we stay focused on the problem the larger and more difficult it becomes.

The Bible tells us that we can do nothing without God.

God has unlimited power and wisdom.

He is always ready and willing to provide a solution to our problems. We just need to ask and believe He will provide an answer. He does not want us to try to work out our problems by ourselves. He wants us to turn them over to Him and trust that He is still in control and wants to help us in our time of need.

Sherry

Day Nine

Humor For The Day

Shawn, my son, came home sad from his first day in first grade. I asked "What did you learn today in school ?"

He said, "Nothing, and the teacher said I had to come back."

Day Nine

Health Tip For The Day

We know that berries and green vegetables are all
superfoods. Sometimes these are the only
superfoods we have in our diet.

You may want to add Alfalfa Sprouts to your diet as it
is another superfood.

They have few calories and no fat or sodium.
They are loaded with antioxidants and have been
reported to help lower cholesterol.

Day Ten

John 8:12
I am the Light of the world. Whoever follows Me will never walk in darkness but have the Light of Light.

It seems that the light of the world is growing dim. We have violence in our streets and the whole world is in a state of violence.

Many people are feeling hopeless and are falling into despair.

We need to believe that God is still at work and can restore our hope.

We can keep hope alive by trusting in God. We serve a mighty God that can do anything.

Jesus brings light into the darkness. He can restore our hope and bring peace when there is unrest.

Sherry

Day Ten

Humor For The Day

My friend, Christine, celebrated her 77th birthday by
going Zip Lining. She is planning to go Sky Diving on her 80th birthday.

And here I am on my birthday feeling good about myself because I got my legs through my jeans without
losing my balance and blowing the candles out without fainting.

Day Ten

Health Tip For The Day

According to Dr. Becker from Bio Innovations, Olive leaf has many health benefits.

Olive leaf lowers blood pressure and improves cholesterol.

It also supports weight management.

It is beneficial for type 2 diabetes, and Olive leaf will help build a strong immune system

Day Eleven

Psalms 22:8

I trust in You, Lord, so I'll let You rescue me.
Teach me to delight in You and deliver me, O God.

You give me Your Shield of Victory, and Your
right hand sustains me.
You stoop down to make me great.
You broaden the path beneath me, so that my
ankles do not turn.
Arm me with strength for the battle, make my
adversary bow down at my feet. Make my enemy
turn back in flight.
Thank You God!
One day You will utterly destroy my foe!
Lord God, I will shout for joy when You make me
victorious, and I will lift a banner in the name of
my God!
Please Lord, grant these requests.
Though my enemy plots evil against me and
devises evil schemes, he will not succeed if I am
walking with You, O God. You will make him turn
back when You aim at him with drawn bow.
Be exalted, O Lord, in Your strength!
I will sing and praise Your might.

Haley

Day Eleven

Humor For The Day

How do I know when I've been in college too long?

When my mom and dad are running out of money.

What did the buffalo say to his son when he left for college"

Bi-son

What do you call a college student who is hiking across the country?

The walking debt.

Day Eleven

Health Tip For The Day

To help your carrots last longer remove the tops.
Store the carrots in a plastic bag in the
refrigerator.
This will help them stay fresh for about two
weeks.
You carrots will store better if you keep them
away
from apples to prevent bitterness.
Carrots will blend well with many healthy foods.
A few of my favorites are stir fry and pasta
salads.

Day Twelve

Hebrew 13:8

Jesus Christ is the same yesterday, today and forever.

We go through seasons of change in our life span. I know that I have had a lot of changes take place in my life over the years. Some changes have been good while other changes have been very painful.

Our world is going through many changes. We have to wear face masks. Many restaurants and small businesses are closed due to Covid-19.

We will continue to experience many changes throughout our life time.

One thing we can be sure of is that God never changes.

He will be with us through every change.

Our church choir sings a song by Matt Redman. It talks about how God will never let go. He is always with us in the storms.

God is just a prayer away.

Another song by The McKameys, talks about how God is with us in the bad times as well as in the good times.

The next time you are in a storm trust God to see you through the storm.

He never changes. He is always there to help.

Sherry

Day Twelve

Humor For The Day

The young man was going to his girlfriend's house to meet her parents.

He stopped by the candy shop to buy some chocolates.
He told the clerk that he wanted a 1 pound, a 3 pound and a 5 pound box of chocolate.

The sales clerk was curious and asked "What are you going to do with all that chocolate?"

The young man explained " I am going to my girlfriend's house and if she lets me hold her hand she gets the 1 pound box, if she lets me put my arm around her she gets the 3 pound box and if she lets me kiss her she gets the 5 pound box of chocolates.

Later that evening he went to dinner. The family gathered around the table and asked the young man to bless the food.

He prayed for the food. He prayed for the missionaries.
He prayed and prayed and prayed, finally he said amen.

His girlfriend said "I didn't know that you were so religious."

He replied"I didn't know that your dad was the candy clerk either."

Day Twelve

Health Tip For The Day

According to Health Line, Green Tea is loaded with antioxidants.

Green Tea nay also aid in weight loss.

It also promotes digestive health.

It can also help your skin have a wonderful glow.

My favorite Green Tea is Matcha.

I like loose tea because it is made from the first crop of leaves and is said to be healthier than tea bags.

Tea bags are made from the left over leaves and are smaller.

Day Thirteen

Joshua 24:15
Choose you this day whom you will serve.

When my grandson died I was devastated. I felt that God had failed me. I prayed and prayed for my grandson to live. I believed with all my heat that he would live.

When he died I became very angry with God. With each passing day my hurt and anger grew to where I did not want anything to do with God.

Weeks later my husband wanted to get away for a few days.

We went to the Amish Country and stayed in a cabin.

I could not sleep that first night . I was sitting in a oversize rocking chair telling God how hurt and angry I was with Him.

I cried and cried until I had no more tears left.

In the stillness of the night I sat there thinking that I would turn my back on God.

Suddenly I realized that I had nothing to go back to. It was as if I was at a crossroad in my life.

I had to choose to turn away from God or move forward.

I thought about my life before God. It was a mess and full of sin. I had nothing to turn back to.

I chose that night to move forward and I asked God to forgive me of all the bad things I had said out of anger and hurt.

I knew that from that day forward I would always follow God. I would trust Him in the bad times as well as in the good times.

Perhaps you are at the crossroad. If you are I pray that you will choose this day to serve God.

Day Thirteen

Humor For The Day

When my boys were younger I would give them a game or a movie.

I would then tell them, mommy is going to talk to Jesus.

On one of these times I was praying and there was a knock on the door.

My oldest son, Shawn said "Mommy, could you ask Jesus to wait a minute, I need to ask you something?"

Day Thirteen

Health Tip For The day

I read this in Woman's World Magazine.

It said that coffee drinkers live 10% longer than non-coffee drinkers.
It also stated that this goes for decaf drinkers also.
The reason they gave for the longer life span was that coffee has lots of nutrients that helps fight off free radicals.

So, go have that second cup of Joe, it just might impact your health!

Day Fourteen

2 Timothy 1:7
For God has not given us the spirit of fear, but of power, and of love and of a sound mind.

Have you ever been afraid of telling someone about Jesus.

I struggle with sharing Jesus with others. I am always worried about what people will think of me.

I think that many Christians are afraid to share Jesus. We are afraid of being rejected. As painful as rejection can be we do not need to let it stop us from sharing Jesus.

As Christians we are called to be witnesses. We are to share what Jesus has done in our lives.

In 1st John the Bible tell us that fear has torment. We do not have to do it on our own as we have The Holy Spirit to help us share. As we depend on The Holy Spirit's Power we can bring others to Him.

We can use our own experiences in telling what Jesus has done for us. Sometime our very actions of how we live for Jesus can be a witness and a testimony that could help heal a broken spirit.

As Christians Jesus has given us an assignment to share Him with others.

We need to ask The Holy Spirit to help us overcome our fear so we can win souls for Him.

Haley

Day Fourteen

Humor For The Day

Do you know why teachers wear sunglasses in the classroom?

Because they have very bright students!

Do you know where door maker's get their education?

From the school of hard knocks.

Day Fourteen

Health Tip For The Day

According to Health Line, Almond Butter is
the healthiest nut butter.
It has 7 grams of protein in 2 tablespoons.
It has a high content of fat but it is a good
fat.
It is said to help with weight loss in spite
of the high fat content.
It has Vitamin E, Magnesium and Calcium.
Almond Butter is on my list of foods to enjoy.

I still enjoy peanut butter from time to time.

Day Fifteen

Luke 10:2
The harvest is plentiful but the laborers are few.

My husband loves to fish and I love the excuses he makes when he comes home with no fish.

A few of my favorites are:

I used the wrong bait.

It's too cold for the fish to bite.

We all make excuses sometimes as to why we can't serve the Lord. I know that over the years I sure had my share of excuses.

The Bible tells us about men that used all kinds of excuses as to why they could not serve God and do what He asked them.

Moses at the burning bush told God who am I to go and bring the Israelites out.

Jeremiah used the excuse that he could not speak for he was a child.

If God is asking you to do service for Him give up that excuse.

God will not ask you to do something and not help you complete it.

God will be with you in all that you do for Him.

God intends for Christians to serve. Serving God is much greater than anything we can gain by making excuses.

Sherry

Day Fifteen

Humor For The Day

When I was teaching first grade, Zack,
one of my students was try to go to sleep.
I walked over to his desk and said
"Zack, you know that you can't sleep
in my class."

Zack replied " I know I can't Mrs Tarlton,
you talk too loud and it keeps me awake!"

Day Fifteen

Health Tip For The Day

In a seminar I had attended I learned that taking fish oil and eating leafy greens could reduce your chances of having heart problems.

Another healthy thing you can do for your heart is eat garlic. You crush two or three cloves to flavor your meals on a daily basis.

My husband is allergic to garlic so I cook my food separately and then add the garlic.

I suggest you use your garlic daily and always keep your breath mints handy.

Day Sixteen

Nehemiah 8:10

The Joy of the Lord is my strength.

It has been said that your cup of joy is only as deep as your cup of sorrows.

There is no question that life is difficult at times.

John 16:33 reminds us that in this world we will have troubles. He tells us to be of good cheer for Jesus has overcome the world.

Joy should not depend on our circumstances. We should enjoy the journey here on Earth.

The Bible tells us that our lives are like a vapor. True joy comes when we realize that God is still in control of every area of our lives.

The next time you find yourself in a storm try to weather out the storm with His Joy.

Sherry

Day Sixteen

Humor For The Day

When I was teaching summer school, one
of my students was caught cheating.
When I confronted him about his cheating,
he asked "How did you know?"
I responded "Because on question four
Bill put down, I don't know and on your
paper you wrote, me neither."

Day Sixteen

Health Tip For The Day

Bananas are full of Potassium and only have 100 calories for a medium banana.

Look for skin that is yellow and blemish free.

Store bananas at room temperature until they get ripe.

Once they are ripe store them in the refrigerator to prevent further ripening. The skin will turn black but the banana will remain fresh.

You can freeze bananas and use them to make shakes or smoothies.

Bananas also go well in fruit salads.

My favorite use for bananas is in breads and muffins.

Yum! Yum!

Day Seventeen

1st Peter 5:7

Cast all your cares upon God, for He cares for you.

God knew that we would face troubles in our life time.
The Bible tells us how to handle our problems, or challenges as my husband prefers to call them.

In my earlier days of being a Christian I worried about something every day.

I know that there was a time I worried so much the only thing holding me together was my hair spray.

I worried and stressed so much that I started having panic attacks.

God taught me not to just cope with my problems but to lean on Him.

I have learned to cast my cares on Him.

We can only see what is happening at the moment but God sees the big picture.

When troubles come into your life don't be afraid. Cast your cares on God and trust that He will take care of the problem, or challenge.

Sherry

Day Seventeen

Humor For The Day

What does stars and false teeth have in common?

They both come out at night!

You know that you are old when the candles
cost more than the cake!

I invited my elderly neighbor to go shopping
and she said

"Honey I am at that age where my back
goes out more than I do."

Day Seventeen

Health Tip For The Day

I grew up eating oats for breakfast.
Have you ever wondered what the difference
is between old fashioned and quick oats.
The only difference is the size of the flakes.
Quick oat flakes are cut in smaller pieces
so they will cook faster.
There is no difference in their nutritional
value.
Steel cut oats are even healthier than old
fashioned or quick oats.
Steel cut oats are minimally processed and
they contain more fiber, making them a
healthier choice for breakfast.

Day Eighteen

James 5:16

The effectual fervent prayer of a righteous man availeth much.

We all have heard how there is power in prayer. When Christians call upon God it can change situations.

Prayer should be our first line of defense when we are battling a storm.

My friend Michele taught me how to pray and trust God in every situation in life. We would meet on a regular basis and pray for our families and the lost world and for revival in our churches.

Over the years I have seen many changes in how God answered our prayers.

Michele had a music ministry and God called her to another church. I was sad and missed our prayer times together.

We stayed in touch and I am so thankful that she taught me how to pray.

God eventually called me to the same church that Michele goes to.

We both have our ministry at our church and we marvel at all the things that God is doing in our lives and the life of our church.

There is nothing God cannot do when we call upon Him for help.

Sherry

Day Eighteen

Humor For The Day

When my son, Barry was four years old
he came into the kitchen the same time I
finished sweeping the floor.
I asked Barry to hold the dust pan for me.
He was happy to help me.
He held the dust pan and I swept all the dirt
into the pan.
I told Barry to dump the dust pan.
He gave me a puzzled look and I told him again
"Barry dump the dust pan."
He dumped the dirt right back onto the floor.
I guess I didn't make myself clear on where
I wanted him to dump the dirt.

Day Eighteen

Health Tip For The Day

Good news for popcorn lovers.
Studies show that snacking on fiber filled
popcorn can lessen their knee pain.
The fiber helps to speed the inflammation
compounds out of your body.
Adults who eat a lot of fiber have 60% less
knee pain than those who eat little fiber.
So pop some popcorn but hold the butter.

Day Nineteen

Proverbs 3:5
Trust in the Lord with all your heart and lean not on your own understanding.

When my husband was hit by a drunk driver that crippled him for life, I was a new Christian and my faith was not strong.

We had many challenging years and I remember telling God "I don't understand why we have to go through this tragedy."

As my faith grew over the years and I looked back I learned many things about trusting God, even though I did not understand it all at the time.

My husband got saved two years after the accident. It has been years since that time and he is still crippled.

All these years I have never heard him question God or ask why?

I too have learned to trust God in things in life even when I don't understand why.

We both trust God and know that He is in control of our lives.

Sherry

Day Nineteen

Humor For The Day

We were taking a summer drive through
the country.
My husband saw this man out standing
in a field.
We kept driving around to see the different
farms.
On our way home we passed the same man
standing in the same field.
My husband was curious. He stopped and
asked the man "Are you okay? Do you need
help?"
The farmer said "No thank you. I am trying
to win a Noble Peace Prize. I heard that they
give it to people who are out standing in their
field!"

Day Nineteen

Health Tip For The Day

Who knew that eating Tuna could make
 you happy!
According to Psychiatry Research, you can
eat 3 ounces of Tuna 3 times a week to cheer
you up.
It contains Omega 3 that helps boost Serotonin
levels.
So, eat your Tuna and get happy.

 I prefer wild caught salmon from Alaska.

Day Twenty

1st Thessalonians 5:11
Encourage one another and build each other up.

We all like to hear and receive compliments. They are very encouraging.

One of the best compliments I received was from a dear friend, Virgil. He has been dead for several years but I still remember his compliment like it was yesterday.

We were in church and I was in a pew behind him. He turned around to shake my hand and said "I want to thank you." I asked "What did I do?"

He said "I want to thank you for just being you."

A principal at one of the schools where I was teaching taught me to start a "Rainy Day File."

In that file I would put every encouraging note I received from the parents of my students.

When I would have a discouraging day I would read from my "Rainy Day Files."

It always made me feel better.

Encouragement was a big part of the early church. As Christians we should encourage each other.

Not encouragement like"Your hair is cute," etc.

Our encouragement should be done with hopes of lifting their hearts toward The Lord.

Sherry

Day Twenty

Humor For The Day

My sister, Darlene has purple hair.
We were walking out of Walmart one day
when this man stopped us.
He said "Did you girls steal my crayons?"
We were not sure what he meant then he
asked again if we had stolen his crayons.
He said "My purple crayon is missing."
Darlene still has her purple hair.

Day Twenty

Health Tip For The Day

You should keep fresh tomatoes at room
temperature.
This will enhance their flavor.

To freeze tomatoes, blanch them for
2 minutes in boiling water, then quickly
put them ice water and drain them.

Tomatoes will add color and flavor to
soups and salads.
I even like to add them to my omelet.

Day Twenty One

Proverbs 3:6
In all thy ways acknowledge Him, and He will direct your path.

I have been praying for a while that God would make me more desperate to know Him more.

This life is not my own, and I want to start living like it.

I feel like He is slowly bringing me to a place of surrender.

It has come to my attention that I push my love for God to the back-burner almost to the point where I'm not ready for people to see Him in me until I get to know them.

As if proclaiming, I love Jesus, is a safe way to get to know people. I fear that part of me will turn others away.

What a ridiculous way to live! Christ is in me and all of me, not part of my life but the whole thing.

Today I had a job interview for a position I was pretty excited about and as I was praying about it the thought came "God please don't let me say anything too churchy,
or something that would mess it up."

Then I realized that I can't live hiding the best part of my life. So, I switched to saying "Lord, don't let me hide You from them, speak through me, and work it out the way You would have it."

That change gave me much more freedom, and when they asked me to tell about myself, the first thing that came out was that I love Jesus.

It was slightly intimidating to speak those words, but I had peace about it and would not change it.

Lord, continue to grow me in a relationship with You.
Live through me and remove my fear and hesitation so that I will serve You openly as a flashing beacon of Your Love and Salvation.

Haley

Day Twenty One

Humor For The Day

I was at a very small mission church
one Sunday.
Everything was very quiet as we heard
the preacher praying.
The silence was broken by a cell phone
ringing.
A little boy spoke up and said
"Mom that better be God!"

Day Twenty One

Health Tip For The Day

My dad used to say that a chicken in every pot meant prosperity.

However in our world today chicken is a symbol of health.

Most doctors recommend that you eat more chicken and less red meat.

Chicken is a better source to lower your cholesterol levels.

Chicken is also good for a low calorie diet. It is healthier and lower in fat if you remove the skin.

Chicken, if stored in the coldest part of your refrigerator will last for two days.

You can freeze chicken and it will last up to six months.

Be sure to wrap the chicken in freezer paper and store in an airtight container.

If your chicken is whole and has giblets then freeze the giblets separately.

Day Twenty Two

Psalms 107:27

They reel to and fro, and stagger like a drunk man, and are at their wit's end.

Have you ever been at your wit's end? Unfortunately I have been there more times than I like to count.

One day I was reading this verse and said "God that's exactly how I feel today."

Oh , I don't mean staggering like a drunk but at my wit's end.

It was one of those times when problems kept popping up and I could not resolve them.

I felt helpless and ready to throw in the towel.

Then I stumbled on Hebrews 4:12 and it talked about how powerful the Word is. It said that It is sharper than a two-edged sword.

I meditated on this verse. How it was quick and sharp and powerful.?

I recalled a scene from Star Wars where Luke Sky Walker had that dramatic fight with Darth Vader.

I started imagining The Holy Spirit using God's Word like a sword to battle my problems.

The Word is sharper than any two-edged sword!

The next time you are at your wit's end, let The Holy Spirit fight your battles.

Sherry

Day Twenty Two

Humor For The Day

I used to teach a Sunday school class.
We would go to the big church, as we
  called it.
We had songs and prayer and after the
  prayer I would take my class to our
  classroom.
I always asked them to be quiet.
  One time a little girl asked
"Why do we always have to be quiet in church?"
  Tommy spoke up and said
    "Because the big people are sleeping."

Day Twenty Two

Health Tip For The Day

I love to drink tea and have tea parties.
I usually serve a few of my favorite teas.
However I do not serve my Ginger tea
  that I make from the ginger root.
Even though it is one of my favorites I only use
 it when I am sick or a family member is sick.
Ginger tea will help calm an upset stomach.
  It will also help relieve headaches.
  It can relieve nausea.
  It can help relieve congestion associated
    with a common cold.
  Ginger tea made from ginger root is very
    beneficial to your health.

Day Twenty Three

Psalms 37:4
Delight yourself also in the Lord, and He shall give you the desire of your heart.

To be honest, I feel inadequate to be writing a devotional when I have so much learning and growing to do in my life.

A little about me: I'm starting college, a new job and working on aligning my life with what God would have me do.

I have so many dreams, goals and idea's of how I'd like my future to be, but the question I've been presented with lately is " Is this really what God wants for me or is it just what I want?"

Oh Lord, replace my desires with Yours.

Psalms 37:4 keeps coming to mind, "Delight yourself in the Lord, and He will give you the desires of your heart."

I want to be filled with the Mind of Christ, so that everything I do springs from a heart dedicated to pursuing my Savior, a mindset of servanthood and love for others.

Philippians 2:13; For it is God who works in you both to will and to do for His pleasure."

I alone am inadequate, but with Christ through me, I am capable. Not by me but Christ through me.

Haley

Day Twenty Three

Humor For The Day

In high school you can't go to lunch because your not allowed.

In college you can't go to lunch because you can't afford it.

Day Twenty Three

Health Tip For The Day

Cinnamon is a delicious spice that is
probably in every spice rack.
Cinnamon does not only add flavor
to food it also has health benefits.
It helps lower insulin levels in diabetics.
It also helps to improve circulation.
Studies have shown that cinnamon
contains a lot of anti-oxidants which
helps prevent the cause of aging.

Day Twenty Four

Revelation 3:20

Behold I stand at the door and knock, if any man hears My voice and opens the door, I will come in to him and sup with him and he with Me.

I love getting gifts especially the unexpected ones.

This year on my birthday a very special friend traveled over 900 miles to celebrate my birthday with me. I had not expected to see him until next year.

When he knocked at our door I was so shocked that I left him standing at the door.

I ran to tell my husband that Ray was here. My husband asked "Where is he?" I told him I left him standing at the door. He said "Well go let him in."

That was a very special birthday gift and one that I will cherish forever.

I received many gifts on my birthday and I loved all of them.

However my most special gift is eternal life through Jesus Christ!

If God is knocking at your heart's door then don't leave Him standing outside like I did to Ray.

Open up your heart wide and invite Him in and receive
The Gift of Eternal Life!

Sherry

Day Twenty Four

Humor For The Day

My husband and I took a trip to the
Amish Country. I love to visit there and
I enjoy seeing all the horse drawn buggies.
On the back of one buggy was a for sale sign.

The sign read:
"Energy efficient vehicle, runs on grass and oats!"

Day Twenty Four

Health Tip For The Day

Most of us probably consume nuts in our diet, like
walnuts, almonds, pecans and peanuts.
You might want to consider Brazil Nuts.
My Doctor told me to add Brazil Nuts to my diet.
Brazil Nuts have a lot of health benefits.
My Doctor told me to eat three Brazil Nuts a day for the
selenium.
They may also help regulate your thyroid.
They are very nutritious.
Brazil Nuts are also heart healthy.

Day Twenty Five

Isaiah 55:12

You shall go out in joy and be led forth in peace.

We live in a busy world. We move at such a fast pace that we get upset when we are delayed.

It bothers us when someone interrupts our routine that slows us down.

We don't like to wait at traffic lights or in long lines at the grocery store.

We allow so many things to steal our joy and peace.

The devil will do anything he can to rob us of our peace and joy. He knows that if we don't have any peace or joy we don't have any power.

We need to remember that as Christians we have the power of God inside of us.

If we don't have peace and joy on the inside of us then we will not have it on the outside.

When you are not moved by what the devil throws
your way, then you will know that God is in control and you will stand firm.

Don't let circumstances determine your peace and joy.

Sherry

Day Twenty Five

Humor For The Day

Someone sent this to me on Facebook. I hope it makes you smile.

A family went out to eat and their six year old son wanted to bless the food. In a very loud voice he blessed the food and then he said "God I would bless it a lot more if mom buys me ice cream for dessert."

Many people heard his prayer and laughed.

Then one lady at the next table spoke up "That's what wrong with kids today, they don't know how to pray, praying for ice cream is a shame!"

The six year old started crying and said "Mom is God mad at me, I didn't mean to do anything wrong?"

The mother comforted her son.

Later on in the meal a man brought her son an ice cream sundae.

Then he took the lady who made the boy cry a sundae. He sat it down and told her to enjoy the ice cream.

He said "It is good for your soul.!"

Perhaps we all need a little ice cream from time to time.

Day Twenty Five

Health Tip For The Day

Cucumbers are very popular in our country.
They are a member of the gourd family.
We all know that carrots are good for our eyes,
but did you know that cucumbers are good for
our eyes also.
They can help prevent cataracts.
Cucumbers are made up mostly of water,
making
them a good moisturizer for the skin.
Cucumbers are a good source of various vitamins
that will help keep our bones healthy.
The sap from the peel will help calm down a bug
bite or a minor rash.
Just peel and wipe the sap from the peeling
on the bite or rash.

Day Twenty Six

John 15:15

I have called you friends, for everything I have learned from My Father, I have made known to you.

My mom used to tell me that if you have five good friends in life you would be doing well.

I guess that I am blessed as I have many friends.

I have some special friends that have played a significant part in my life.

Faye is my prayer warrior.

Joyce is my health coach.

Christine is my chef.

Janice keeps me encourages.

Opal is the best Uber driver in the world.

They stand with me and help weather the storms.

We all need friends but Jesus is the best friend of all. He will never leave us.

Jesus is a friend even closer than a brother.

Like the song says "What a friend we have in Jesus."

When you have Jesus as a best friend you will always have someone to help you through all your struggles.

Put Jesus at the top of your friend list and call upon him daily.

Sherry

Day Twenty Six

Humor For The Day

My husband joined me in church one Sunday.
The pastor came and shook my husband's hand.
He said
"You need to come and join The Lord's Army."
My husband replied
"I'm already in The Lord's Army."
Then why do I only see you at Christmas and
Easter
the pastor asked?
Terry replied "Because I'm in The Secret
Service."

Day Twenty Six

Health Tip For The Day

Baking Soda has been around for a long time.
We have all used it in one way or other.
You can brush your teeth or wash your clothes
with it.
We all probably have a box in our refrigerator
to help reduce odor's.
You probably already know these uses.
I found a few more uses on the internet.
Baking Soda can be used as a natural deodorant.
It will banish odors without using harsh
chemicals.
You can use it as a dry shampoo when your sick
and
can't use water to wash your hair.
My husband drinks Baking Soda in water every
night
for his heartburn.
He says that it really helps.

Day Twenty Seven

Psalms 9:9

The Lord is a refuge for the oppressed, a stronghold in times of trouble.

All of us have been tempted to give up and throw in the towel. We have a choice to surrender and give up or fight the battle.

It is easy to throw in the towel and give up when we focus more on the problem than on the solution.

We need to focus on God and not on the problem. God wants us to bring all our problems to Him.

Proverbs 3:6 tells us to acknowledge Him in all our ways and He will direct our paths. There is no problem too big or too complicated that God can not handle.

The next time you feel like giving up just stand firm and say "I will never give up or surrender."

Find a scripture that pertains to your challenge and keep repeating it out loud over and over again.

Do not be moved away from what the Bible says about your challenge or by your circumstances.

The devil tries to get us to doubt that God can't fix our problem, but God is faithful and we can trust The Word of God it is impossible for God to lie.

Hebrew 10:23 tells us to hold fast to the confession of our faith without wavering for He who has promised is faithful.

Sherry

Day Twenty Seven

Humor For The Day

In Florida you can fish in freshwater
or fish in saltwater.
There are different kinds of fish in the
freshwater than in the saltwater.
I asked my husband " Why can't they
all live together?"
"Why can't the freshwater fish live in
the saltwater?"
He answered and said "All that salt
would give the freshwater fish
high blood pressure."

Day Twenty Seven

Health Tip For The Day

We all have used pumpkins to decorate with.
We have carved faces on them around
Halloween.
We have pumpkin pie on holidays.
Pumpkin is another one of the superfoods.
It is full of Iron, Zinc and Fiber.
It is high in Vitamin C and Beta Carotene.
Pumpkin is also good for our skin and
 indigestion.

Day Twenty Eight

Matthew 5:16

Let your light shine before men so they can see your good works and glorify your Father which is in Heaven.

Throughout the New Testament Jesus followers were lights in the darkness.

In His word God instructs His people to let their light shine.

We are living in a world of lost people. They want change and hope for the future but are looking for it in all the wrong places.

Those of us who know Jesus realize that true hope comes only from God.

It is important for Christians to shine bright. Let others see the good work that Jesus has done in you.

Always try to see the good in others. Always seize the opportunity to say a kind word to encourage others.

As your light shines on others The Light of Jesus will shine on you.

The more light you allow to shine the brighter your world will become.

Sherry

Day Twenty Eight

Humor For The Day

I am a hearing interpreter for the deaf.
I would go to many events with my deaf
  friends.
My husband would join us occasionally.
We would use sign language as our means
  of communication.
My husband knew very little sign language.
Once, at one of these events, my husband told
  my deaf friend she looked like a pretty pig.
He meant to say she had a pretty dress on.
I asked him not to sign anymore until he
  knew sign language better.

Day Twenty Eight

Health Tip For The Day

Grapes can help with weight loss.
They contain Vitamin K and C.
Grapes are good for inflammation.
Grapes are a heart healthy snack.
Both red and green grapes have
the same health benefits.
Grape juice is also good for you but
it has more sugar than grapes alone.

Day Twenty Nine

Mark 13:23
But take ye heed: behold, I have foretold you all things.

Have you noticed that when you open a pack of seeds they don't look anything like the picture on the package. Like pretty flowers or vegetables.

But, if you put them in the ground they have the potential to produce and look like the pictures.

That is the same way with God's Word. It is a seed and our heart is the soil.

When we read and study the Bible it will produce fruit.

Our life is like a garden where God meant for us to be alive with growth.

Just like a garden, we plant, we must have a good foundation to start with.

It is the same with our spiritual garden and that foundation is Jesus!

We still need to water our spiritual garden with The Word of God daily.

When we put the Word of God into us we will grow into a beautiful vessel for our Lord and Savior.

Sherry

Day Twenty Nine

Humor For The Day

My boy's came running into the
house after school.
They left the front door wide open.
I asked " Okay boys, who was born
in the barn and left the door open?"
My son, Barry replied
"I know mom, it was baby Jesus."

Day Twenty Nine

Health Tip For The Day

Late in the growing season,
due to the cold, it is hard for
tomatoes to ripen.
 Try putting the tomatoes into a
brown paper bag and then put
them in a dark closet.
Check on them daily as it could
take only a few days or up to
a week for them to ripen.

Day Thirty

Psalms 46:10
Be still and know that I am God.

God wants us to have joy in the midst of
   the storms of life.
We have to hear from God when he speaks to us.
God will speak to us in different ways.
He speaks to us through His Word.
He uses music and preaching to speak to us.
I remember one time when I was praying and
needed an
   answer but I didn't hear from God.
When I became quiet, this song came to mind.
   "Have faith in God when your pathway is lonely.
Have faith in God He is on His Throne. Have faith
in God when your prayers are not answered."
I felt that that song was God speaking to me. I
felt that
   God was telling me to listen and to trust Him.
   Sometimes as Christians we can be rude.
Especially
   when we pray and tell God all we have to say
and then leave.
   We should be still and let God speak to us.
   Don't let it be a one sided conversation.
   If God is to teach us we must be still to hear him.

Sherry

Day Thirty

Humor For The Day

Why did the teacher write
on the window?

Because she wanted the lesson
to be clear!

A teacher asked Johnny;
"If you got six dollars from six
of your friends what do you get?"

Johnny replied "A new bike."

Day Thirty

Health Tip For The Day

Almond Milk is lower in calories
 than cow's milk
It is low in sugar and high in
 Vitamin E
It is also a good source of Calcium
 and Vitamin D
Almond Milk is one of the top
selling plant base milk's because
of it's rich texture and flavor.

God Changes Lives.

God can heal the broken-hearted
and set the captive free.
He has changed my life and He can change
Yours too..
It is easy as A B C.

A. Admit that you are a sinner and need to be saved.

B. Believe that Jesus rose from the dead and He has the power to forgive you.

C. Confess that Jesus is your Savior and that He is your Lord.

Romans 10:9
If you confess with your mouth Jesus is Lord
and believe in your heart that God has raised
Him from the dead, you will be saved!

Following are testimonies of how God has
changed lives.

Shoes From God

As Sherry, my wife, and I walked out of the doctor's office we were shocked at the news that we just received.

In November, 2011, I had gone through my second knee replacement surgery. I had just recovered from my first knee surgery.

The first knee surgery went so well that I had decided to have the other knee done.

I had a crushed ankle on the same side as the new surgery and during surgery my ankle was accidentally pulled out of socket.

After six months it was not any better so my doctor sent me to a specialist.

That's when Sherry and I received the devastating news.

After x-ray's and evaluation, the doctor informed us that I would need extensive surgery and rehabilitation that would take me over a year to recover.

He wanted to schedule me immediately for surgery on the crooked Tibia (shin) bone . This first procedure would take four months with no weight on the leg. He also stated that the procedure only had a 50% chance of working.

I asked the doctor

"What if I don't have the operation?"

He said without the operation in three months or less I would not be unable to walk on my ankle.

As I hobbled to the car and we set there in disbelief Sherry said " What are we going to do?"

Trying to be brave and not alarm her I said "We will just have to trust in God." Then we prayed.

Soon after we met our son, Barry, for lunch. As we finished Barry asked if I would drop off some computer parts that he did not need. Then he said "That's ok dad I can do it." I said no, I needed to check on a brace for my ankle at a store near the computer store.

I dropped off the parts and went to check on an ankle brace when I noticed the brace store was closed. I went next door to a shoe store and asked about it.

The owner informed me that the store had closed. He said "I noticed you struggling across the parking lot, what's wrong?"

I explained my situation and he asked me my shoe size.

Then he asked if I would listen to a video while he checked on something.

About this time Sherry came into the store and asked me what I was doing. I said "This man says he can help my ankle!" Sherry looked at me with skepticism as we had been through " miracle " cures before.

The owner put these crazy shoes on, adjusted them and said "Try to walk."I got up and walked to the front of the store and back.

Sherry and I looked at each other in amazement and I said "I can walk with less pain." We both had tears in our eyes.

That was over 8 years ago and I still have my Z-Coil Shoes. I call them, as in Sherry's first book, my God Shoes. I did not have to have the surgery.

God surely knows when, how and where to bless us.

Terry Tarlton

Dog Gone

I love to fox hunt. In order to have a good hunt you have to have good fox dogs.

I had the best fox dogs that I had ever owned. We hunted often.

This one night I lost my fox dogs. I was devastated. I looked the country over for my dogs.

I advertised on the radio that if anyone found my dogs please contact me. I heard nothing and my dogs were still missing.

After six weeks and my dogs were still missing I prayed and asked God to return my dogs and that if He did I would start going to church.

God returned the dogs in the exact place where I had lost them. I did not keep my word and go to church.

God spoke to me and said "Bill I gave you your dogs back and I can take them again."

I would think about God's Word while I was hunting but I still ignored Him.

One night I had a dream that my best and fastest dog was dead. The next morning, when I went to feed my dogs my best dog was missing.

I went looking for my dog and found him in

awell where he had fallen and drowned.

God had got my attention and I started going to church.

I was saved and love my Lord. I still enjoy fox hunting but I love my Lord more than hunting.

Bill Pennington

Redeemed

One of my favorite songs is "Redeemed" by Big Daddy Weave.

I can barely listen to this song without tearing up.

I was a mess when I opened my heart to the Lord. I had a laundry list of problems.

Heavy alcohol use, abusing prescription and sleep medication, marriage in trouble, fear of losing my job and carrying the load of doing things throughout my life that I was ashamed of.

I was to the point of considering suicide. I was in pain.

I cannot express the joy of putting down those chains and I give praise to Jesus for forgiving me of my sins.

I once thought that I was so far gone that even God did not want me.

But I discovered that there is no sin greater than The Blood of Jesus.

He set me free!   **Robbie Dalton**

I Hate Drugs_!_

"I hate drugs." "How could you pick drugs over your family?" "We love you, isn't that enough?"

These are words that I would yell at my, then husband
and father of our two boys as he would walk out of the door leaving us in order to go get high.

I was in constant turmoil. I was shattered and after 10 years I could not do it any more.

We divorced in 2009 and in 2018 he left us again for good as drugs had taken his life. Except this time, instead of anger I felt compassion, why?

Because the same girl who hated drugs years before and just knew it would not happen to her, had faced addiction and had barely made it out alive.

A doctor once told me that there were only three options for an addict who doesn't get help: institution, prison or death. It has also been said "Addiction has no prejudice," and boy aren't those sayings true.

My life appeared to be good to the outsider. I was a registered nurse with a great paying job. I had two handsome and healthy sons. I had a nice home and car, but on the inside I felt empty. I was riddled with anxiety and depression. I felt abandoned and alone. I was tired.

Not long after my divorce I had a bunch of left over pain pills from a previous surgery. I remembered that my ex-husband used to feel energy when he would take an opiate.

I thought that I would try it, one wouldn't hurt! They were prescribed to me, so it was legal. I took it and had so much energy! I cleaned my house. I cooked a good dinner for my kid's. I helped them with their homework. I felt amazing, happy and accomplished after a very long work week. It even helped my chronic back pain. I thought, hey, I'll just take these on my days off to get things done.

I wouldn't need them very long, just a few weeks to get caught up on things.

But two days turned into three and so on until it was every day. Then I ran out of pills.

After a day or two, I remember going to my sister's house and telling her that I was not feeling very well and I thought that I was going through withdraw from those pain pills. Oh, if I had only stopped them!

Shortly after I started having gall bladder issues. The pain was intense. I was put on pain pills and the doses kept getting prescribed higher and higher until my gall bladder was removed.

When every pill ran out it was too late, I was hooked. I needed that feeling and I needed the pills to stop getting sick. It was no longer fun, it was a necessity.

The next four years probably sound like most drug addicts. The pain pills weren't enough anymore so I became addicted to crack cocaine and anything else I could get my hands on.

The years were full of lies, stealing, hurting my family and friends, body racked with sickness until

I could get my next fix.

I lost friends, my home, my job, my license and eventually, after a suicide attempt, I nearly lost my life.

I grew up in a Christian home. I love The Lord. I had experienced His Love and Presence many times .

Even during addiction I felt guilt and shame because I knew what I was doing was wrong but it wasn't enough and most of the times I didn't care and when I did I would just use more to numb the pain.

I felt that God would never forgive me. I was too broken, too far gone and a lost cause. I had seen and done too much, but I was wrong!

The fervent prayers of my family did not go unanswered. God is faithful. He will never leave or forsake you.

I started small. ("Do not despise these small beginnings, for the Lord rejoices to see the work done." **Zechariah 4:10**

My dad began to have a weekly Bible study with me and I began to watch a Christian T.V. Show that intrigued me and left me wanting more.

I started reading the Bible and His Word transformed me.

He says seek Me and you will find me and when I found Him again I was forever changed. Jesus is in love with us. He had never left me. He was always there.

Now I walk in His love. I feel joy like never

before. He has restored all that I had lost.

I am now in a ministry that helps other addicts. Nothing brings me more joy than to see others set free!

My walk with The Lord has been a journey, but oh my, how it has been such a beautiful one!

"If you remain in Me and My Word's remain in you,ask whatever you wish, and it will be given unto you." **John 15:7**

Jamie Endicott

www.ingramcontent.com/pod-product-compliance
Lightning Source LLC
Chambersburg PA
CBHW071610040426
42452CB00008B/1308